THE EARLY YEARS
Career Development for Young Children

A Guide for Parents/Guardians

Mildred Cahill
Edith Furey

Copyright © Cahill, M. (2017)

Published by:
CERIC
Foundation House
Suite 300, 2 St. Clair Avenue East
Toronto, ON
M4T 2T5
Website: www.ceric.ca
Email: admin@ceric.ca

ISBN
Paperback: 978-1-988066-23-3
ePDF: 978-1-988066-24-0

In collaboration with: Cahill, M. and Furey, E., Memorial University of Newfoundland

The Early Years: Career Development for Young Children
A Guide for Parents/Guardians

Design and layout: Alison Carr Design & Typogrphay (www.alisoncarr.ca)

The following photographs courtesy of www.istockphoto.com:

p. 6: istock.com/ lewkmiller   p. 31: istock.com/David Sacks
p. 14: istock.com/Image Source   p. 36: istock.com/JBryson;
p. 16 and 26: istock.com/FatCamera   p. 38: istock.com/tatyana_tomsickova
p. 19: istock.com/andresr   p. 40: istock.com/omgimages
p. 23 and 35: istock.com/monkeybusinessimages   p. 41: istock.com/kiankhoon
p. 25: istock.com/Yagi-Studio   p. 43: istock.com/SeanShot

Photographs on pages 5, 11, and 18 courtesy of Angela Stewart and Amanda Mullins
Photographs on pages 8, 9, 10, 15, 21, 30, 35 (top left), and 44 courtesy of Sabrina Kelsey
Cover photograph courtesy of istock.com/FatCamera

This material may be used, reproduced, stored, or transmitted for non-commercial purposes. However, the author's copyright is to be acknowledged. It is not to be used, reproduced, stored, or transmitted for commercial purposes without written permission from CERIC. Every reasonable effort has been made to identify the owners of copyright material reproduced in this publication and to comply with Canadian Copyright law. The publisher would welcome any information regarding errors or omissions.

All photos in this guide are for illustrative purposes only. They are not actual photos of any individuals mentioned.

Contents

Preface 5

Research study of career development: An overview 7

Career development for young children: What is it?...................... 9

Influences on career development 12

How do parents/guardians support and enhance children's development
    of self? 13

How do parents /guardians support and enhance children's interests
    and abilities? 17

How do parents/guardians support and enhance children's development of
    healthy relationships? 23

How do parents/guardians support and empower children to adjust to change,
    make decisions, and solve problems?.............................. 28

How do parents/guardians support and empower children to participate in
    family and community life?....................................... 33

How do parents/guardians influence children's aspirations for future selves?.............. 37

How do parents/guardians enhance children's knowledge of diverse work
    roles in families and communities? 42

Highlights 47

Note to parents/guardians... 48

References 49

Acknowledgements 51

Preface

Today's workplace is dynamic and ever changing, filled with a dazzling array of diverse opportunities for work and employment for youth. However, many young people experience difficulty navigating their way through a career path that fulfills their needs. Parents[1] wonder how to support the career development of their children.

Typically, youth and young adults are the ones concerned with the serious questions about career development and the future. Yet the roots of career development begin early in a child's life. What do we mean when we talk about career development for young children?

Adults will often reflect back to their own childhoods as the early beginnings of their interests and abilities. For adults, career development is about the past (their childhood), the present, and the future. For children, it's all about their present lives and their dreams for the future. These dreams are often based in fantasy, but are very real to children.

As children mature physically, they are growing socially and learning to relate to other siblings, family, peers, and playmates. So too, they are developing cognitively, increasing their critical thinking skills and formulating their values, ideas, and preferences. Career development for young children (preschool, primary, and early elementary) is about helping them in the here-and-now, the present, to

---

1. In this document, *parents* refers to *parents/guardians*.

- Is it too early (ages three to eight years) to think about career development?
- How is career development different from child development?
- How do children learn about work through play?

develop a healthy sense of self and the competencies that will enable them to reach their full potential. Children of the future will have the same biological, social, emotional, and educational expectations of children of the past and present, but their worlds will be very different.

In our research, we set out to determine what, if any, knowledge young children (ages three through eight years) had of career and work behaviors and concepts. We engaged with parents and educators[2] through focus groups and surveys and asked them what they thought about young children's awareness of career development concepts. Parents responded to questions, such as: Who is today's child? How can I assist my child? How do I help create a healthy future for my child?

Ignoring the process of career development occurring in childhood is similar to a gardener disregarding the quality of the soil in which a garden will be planted.

—Niles & Harris-Bowlsbey, 2017, p. 276

---

2 In this document, *educators* refers to *pre-school* and *primary teachers, early childhood educators,* and *day-care workers.*

From this work, we compiled data from all three groups; children, parents, and educators. We sifted through those focus groups and surveys and put together rich findings. We then carefully examined the literature to compare our findings with what had already been compiled by earlier researchers and writers.

The most exciting aspect about our study was that we obtained evidence from the children that the seeds of career development were apparent. They were interested in various activities, doing chores and the work of adults, and were quite capable of sharing their hopes and dreams.

This booklet is one of the products we developed based on our research findings. The information presented here is intended for parents to reflect upon career development and young children in the here-and-now. It is not a guide to proper parenting. We believe that parents are the experts on their children. This booklet presents parents' and children's perspectives about young children as they grow and make sense of their world, which includes the family, community, school, work, interests, hobbies, values, and preferences. This booklet is not meant to be followed in order — all themes, while presented as separate sections are interconnected and flow into each other.

Research Study of Career Development: An Overview

This booklet has resulted from a research study conducted from 2014 to 2016 on young children's career development (ages three to eight years). The study aimed to understand the process and nature of young children's career development. The ideas and information contained within came from surveys completed by parents and educators as well as from focus group meetings with children, educators, and parents.

In our research study, 1194 parents and 136 educators completed surveys. Focus groups were held with 436 children, ages three to eight years old, and with 41 parents and 51 educators of children, ages three to eight years.

Survey questions explored parents' understanding of, and their attitudes and beliefs about, the context and developmental process of young children's career development. Questions sought information about parents' perceptions of how they intentionally and unintentionally influenced their children's career development in essential career development areas of self-confidence, self-esteem, decision-making and problem-solving, attitudes towards work and school, and personal aspirations. The focus groups with parents complemented information obtained from the surveys, and provided opportunities for more in-depth discussion, reflection, and examination of their perceptions of children's career development.

In the focus group meetings with young children, we set out to examine children's knowledge and attitudes regarding career development. Through the medium of art and storytelling, children were

provided with opportunities to illustrate and express: their interests, hobbies, and extracurricular activities; knowledge and attitudes towards work, including awareness of their parents' and significant others' work; and their personal dreams for future selves; as well as their contributions to families and communities.

Throughout this booklet, we emphasize the important role that parents play in their children's career development. We have shared examples of parents' understandings and descriptions of children's career development, as well as how they support and influence it. In addition, children's stories about real life experiences and relationships are told. Parents' and children's stories are provided to help guide parents in the important process of supporting their children's career development. As the topics throughout this booklet illustrate, children's career development is not a structured, preplanned process whereby children are taught about jobs, work, and careers. Instead, we invite you on a journey of reflection on the many ways in which you already support and influence your children's future aspirations and career decisions.

It is our hope that the shared stories, real-life experiences, attitudes, and opinions of children, parents, and educators will guide you as you assist your young child in career development.

Career development for young children: What is it?

Career development, like other kinds of development (e.g., physical development, emotional development) is a lifelong process. Career development is not just about jobs, work, and careers, rather it is about life stories. Children actively explore their worlds and begin to construct possibilities for present and future selves. These life stories include a sense of self (self-identity), life roles, skills, and knowledge, and are shaped by everyday events and experiences, as well as by interests, attitudes, beliefs, and role models.

Through play, children explore their environments as they move through various life roles (child, student, adolescent, worker, parent, and others) and adapt skills to cope with educational, career, and personal tasks. The roots of adaptability start early in children's development and play a large part throughout their life adjustment and career planning, and are ingredients of risk-taking, problem-solving, decision-making/planning, transitions and change, and overcoming obstacles and setbacks.

From a very young age, children envision themselves in possible roles for future selves. Children talk about, express, and 'try on' their hopes and dreams for the future. These aspirations change often and are influenced by many factors, including:
- Relationships with parents, educators, peers, and significant others
- Interests, experiences, hopes, and dreams
- TV, media, and play
- Education/learning, knowledge, and skills

Hopes and dreams for future roles vary from fantasy to reality, reflect traditional and non-traditional roles, and stereotypical and non-stereotypical gender roles. As children age and mature, they develop a greater sense of control over their futures. Children benefit from making choices regarding many aspects of their lives, including decisions about experiences, play, friends, peer groups, foods to eat, and clothes to wear.

Children's sense of control over their futures is shaped and supported by positive role models. When they feel safe and secure in their environments, they develop a positive sense of self and become more secure about taking healthy risks. They overcome obstacles and setbacks as they receive support and encouragement. This in turn fuels their belief in self and willingness to persevere and work through difficulties to achieve goals.

Children, by nature, are curious and inquisitive about experiential, educational, career, and work options. They have countless dreams and hopes that reflect diversity of interests in nature, art, learning, and people in their adult worlds. Worlds of fantasy and heroes who are mythical are sometimes interchanged with reality and real-life people.

Children have an awareness of their parents' and significant others' work roles; this awareness increases and broadens as children age. Children are exposed to career, work, and jobs in many ways, including, media, TV, books, games, and other everyday life activities and experiences. They are aware that adults work, and can also discuss work and jobs for which they have responsibility (putting toys away, looking after clothes, cleaning up, helping with gardening, looking after pets, etc.).

From an early age, children often identify with workers in their immediate environments, for example, clerks, bus drivers, teachers, doctors, truck drivers, community workers, and the occupations of their parents and various family members. Children care about their world and are excited about exploring what adults do in various jobs and roles.

As children develop self-identity, interests, and skills, they begin to envision themselves in various career roles. Age-appropriate experiences and reinforcement from loving, caring adults help foster a positive self-identity, often manifested through development of confidence and risk-taking skills. When adults encourage and support children day-to-day, they are nurtured, and are sustained in their love of learning, natural curiosity, and belief in self.

The next part of this guide book is divided into seven sections based on emerging themes:
- How do parents/guardians support and enhance children's development of self?
- How do parents/guardians support and enhance children's interests and abilities?
- How do parents/guardians support and enhance children's development of healthy relationships?
- How do parents/guardians support and empower children to adjust to change, make decisions, and solve problems?
- How do parents/guardians support and empower children to participate in family and community life?
- How do parents/guardians influence children's aspirations for future selves?
- How do parents/guardians support and enhance children's knowledge of diverse work roles in families and communities?

The themes emerged from data obtained from children, parents and educators in our study on children's career development. These themes are not intended to be separate and distinct, but rather should be considered as interrelated and connected. A healthy sense of identity, self-efficacy, and self-awareness are integral to all of these themes. Each section includes commentary based on research findings, as well as direct quotes from participants.

The first ten years of life have been called, correctly, the "nursery of human nature." This is the period of life when a child's goals, achievement motivation, and perception of selves as worthy or inferior begin to be formulated. The concepts children acquire during this life stage directly influence later school success, career identity, adult interests, and general perspectives on life as their attitudes about success and failure develop early.

—Herr, Cramer & Niles, 2004, p. 343

Influences on Career Development

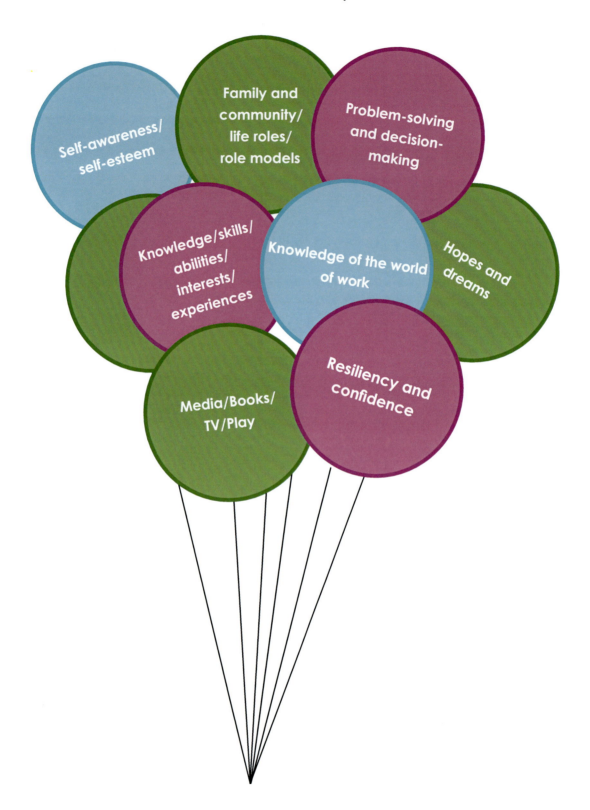

How do parents/guardians support and enhance children's development of self?

At a glance

- How children feel about themselves (self-esteem) and how confident they are in their abilities (self-efficacy) is influenced by many factors.
- Parents have the greatest influence on children's self-esteem and self-confidence.
- Children who have positive self-esteem and self-efficacy are able to initiate and maintain healthy relationships with others.
- When children feel confident, they try new tasks, and become more motivated and engaged in learning.

Children's beliefs about themselves and their ability to learn and master new skills and challenges begin in early childhood. These beliefs are not fixed; rather they are dynamic and ever changing. These beliefs require nurturing throughout life as the child grows, changes, and adapts to different experiences.

Children's beliefs about themselves are shaped by their interests and abilities. They discover who they are and who they can become as they play, explore, and indeed, master their environments.

More importantly, children's beliefs are influenced by experiences and events, and through support and feedback from interactions and relationships within the family, school, and community (including peers). With positive experiences and feeling loved and valued, children adapt, adjust, and thrive socially, emotionally, and cognitively; they develop healthy self-concepts and the confidence to try out and master everyday challenges.

At home and in school, children learn to follow age-appropriate rules, cooperate with peers and siblings, and over time, acquire work habits (e.g., doing homework and helping tidy up). As higher expectations are applied, children step up to meet challenges that can either build or decrease their self-confidence.

> **Parents, schools, peers, and the larger communities are interconnected, and play important roles in the building of children's beliefs about themselves (self-efficacy and self-esteem).**

Children know what they like; sometimes they need encouragement to do things. (parent)

In our study, parents recognized the important role they play in helping their children develop

Career Development for Young Children 13

VIGNETTE

Learning to tie laces is a complex skill and can be frustrating for many children. When Ava started to tie the laces in her runners, Dad watched for signs of frustration. When Ava started to scrunch up her nose, Dad knew that it was time to intervene. He said, "Good work, Ava, I can tell you're trying hard. You made the first knot and you're well on your way. It's not easy to learn to tie laces, it takes lots of practice." Ava's Dad is encouraging Ava's efforts, and hence, increasing her self-confidence and willingness to persist.

positive beliefs about themselves (self-efficacy and confidence) and to become caring, innovative and engaged citizens of the world. When children receive age-appropriate support from adults and peers, they are more likely to succeed and thrive in their current and future education/careers.

Parents want their children to be happy and feel a sense of positive well-being. How do parents support this development? The majority of parents in our study felt that their children were confident in trying new things. Parents' responses reflected a belief in their children's ability to solve problems on their own, try new things, and adapt to change. Parents believed that their children have high levels of resiliency; when they make mistakes they will try again and bounce back from adversity.

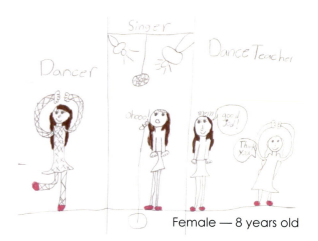

Female — 8 years old

She wants to be a dancer, dance teacher, and famous singer. She likes dancing and she takes lessons.

My granddaughter was really shy, but her parents are exposing her to lots of activities, and now she is becoming more outgoing. (grandparent)

They need role models they can look up to and who are open to new things. (parent)

He loves playing soccer with his Dad.

Something to think about...

- How do I enable my child to experience success?
- How do I support my child to persist as new skills are learned?
- How do I encourage and reinforce my child's efforts and what my child has learned?
- How do I encourage patience and persistence in my child to complete tasks?

Career Development for Young Children

? What if...

- **?** Your child is attending a skating party at the local arena. Your child has limited experience with skating and is anxious about how he will perform. How do you encourage your child to participate so that he will enjoy the experience with friends?
- **?** Your child is starting school in September and is learning to button her coat. She becomes frustrated when she doesn't succeed on the first or second attempt. How do you encourage her to keep trying and support her efforts while building her self-confidence?
- **?** Your child is playing a board game with her older cousin, who always wins. She becomes angry and refuses to play anymore. How do you help her deal with such situations when she experiences setbacks and frustrations?

16   The Early Years

How do parents/guardians support and enhance children's interests and abilities?

At a glance

- Exposure to a diverse range of activities and interests provide children with knowledge beneficial to their future career development.
- Children love to learn by: exploring things on their own, asking and figuring out their own questions, interacting with others, trying new things, cultivating new interests, mastering new skills, and gaining knowledge.
- It is important for children to not limit or dismiss interests and options.
- Parents are the children's first teachers and continue to nurture children's love of learning through play and in natural settings throughout childhood and beyond.
- It is important to be actively involved and to monitor children's activities.
- Family involvement in children's activities and interests encourages their continued participation.

Young children are highly enthusiastic, curious, and ready to learn. Their interests, likes or preferences, and abilities are central to career development and to their overall well-being and sense of contentment. They provide the early seeds or roots of competence.

As children take on and master activities and build their interests, they develop a sense of accomplishment which improves their self-confidence. As they succeed in areas of interest, they will grow from these positive experiences and become motivated to try new things.

Most parents in the study were tuned into their children's love of learning, and readily talked about their children's specific interests. As well, many of the extracurricular out-of-school and leisure activities or hobbies which children partake in during early childhood sustain them through middle childhood and are linked to their later educational, social, and career preferences. Parents in our study felt that participation in extracurricular activities had a lifelong impact on their children. They felt it supported the development of: team work, social skills, physical development, self-esteem, and self-confidence. According to parents, extracurricular activities are an important part of family life.

My 6 year old daughter likes arts and music. She wants to be a teacher. My three-year-old son likes shapes and numbers. (parent)

All activities are important. The extracurricular activities are important, and involvement in other activities — for example, we take them to The Rooms (museum) for craft activities. (parent)

Career Development for Young Children   17

Children know what they like. Sometimes they need encouragement to do things. They will say that they cannot do something, but we encourage them to try. Our motto is that they always have to try. (parent)

Engagement in leisure roles improves skills and competence, and helps children feel more positive about themselves. Parents in the study observed that as their children practice control over activities and tasks: they build capacity to sustain attention; they engage, and welcome opportunities to problem-solve, make decisions, and be creative; and their competence, self-confidence, self-acceptance, and independence are boosted.

Children's capacity for self-awareness of their ability level increases with age and developmental level. Younger children (ages five and six years) are more optimistic and enthusiastic about their abilities in extracurricular activities and are more likely to rate themselves quite high on various abilities (sports, music, etc.), whereas older children (ages nine and ten years) are less likely to do so. As children experience setbacks and frustration they become more doubtful about their abilities. They will often hesitate to join activities when they feel they will not do as well as their peers. Some parents noted that their children's interests have changed over time and are often influenced by the peer group. Children are more likely to try something new in the company of peers.

Parents in our study noted the importance of supporting and encouraging their children's interests and abilities. Parental expectations for success as well as their continuous praise/reinforcement for effort help children in areas of interest.

While all children across age groups (three to eight years) in our study identified gender-neutral toys and games as of interest to both girls and

Female – 7 years old

She wants to be an artist. She needs to get a high school and university education and to practice her drawing.

18   The Early Years

VIGNETTE

Avi's parents thought that swimming was important. They saw it not only as a worthwhile leisure activity, but also as a life skill that would improve his physical development and safety around water. Avi, however, had a fear of water and was not enthusiastic about enrolling in a swimming program. His parents started reading him books about swimming safety, making bath time more fun, and taking him to the swimming areas in the summer time. Avi's attitude towards swimming became more positive especially when he noticed how much fun his friends were having in the water. Gradually, Avi began to spend more time in the water and is now willing to take swimming lessons. As Avi's swimming abilities improved, his self-confidence and belief in his ability to handle difficult tasks increased. Swimming is now one of his favorite activities!

boys (Minecraft, iPad, video games, painting, board games, and riding bikes), they also demonstrated sensitivity to gender identity and identified gender-specific interests. This was particularly true for the younger children, who were more likely to show gender-stereotyped interests, whereas older children were less likely to demonstrate stereotyped interests. There was some evidence that girls identified interests in such toys as trucks, cars, trains, Super Mario, wrestling, etc. However, there was little evidence of boys identifying interests in such toys as dolls, princesses, My Little Pony, dancing, necklaces, etc.

In our study, most parents felt that children's self-awareness of interests and talents was important in developing their talents and abilities; they connected their children's self-awareness with their awareness of interests and abilities. Some parents viewed their children as highly self-aware, clearly knowing what they liked, their strengths and preferences, while others were less

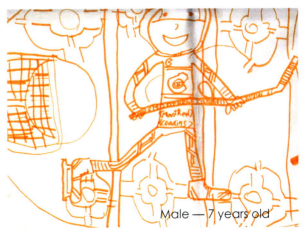

Male — 7 years old

Wants to be a hockey player and play centre ice. His favorite sport is hockey and he plays it now.

Career Development for Young Children   19

confident about their children's self-awareness. Even in the case of siblings, parents remarked differences in interests and abilities.

Through storytelling, artwork, and puppetry, children in the focus groups readily identified their interests, passions, and 'favorites'. These interests and passions represented typical and common interests among children. Children's interests included the following theme areas: games and toys, television shows, movies, books, and activities and sports. As the age of the children increased, so did the quantity and diversity of their interests. Interests often reflected the current season (e.g., snow related activities during winter) and current events and happenings (e.g., soccer identified during the FIFA World Cup).

The three year old will notice that she does not draw as well as her sister and she will say I can't draw that — don't see much of that in the five-year-old. (parent)

Children are influenced by what they see on TV, for example, when Tangled came out they were all doing things from that. (parent)

I find that if she goes with other children, then she will participate and have a good time. It is part of the wanting to fit in, for example, skating, wall climbing. (parent)

Something to think about...

1. How are my child's interests and activities recognized and encouraged?
   - Do I talk to my child about his/her specific interests?
   - Do I provide opportunities for my child to develop interests?
   - Do I participate with my child in his/her interests?

2. How do I support my child in building or constructing his/her own unique identity?
   - Does my child recognize his/her own uniqueness as an individual – for example, how is he/she like and different from others?

3. How is diversity recognized and celebrated within the family and community?

4. How does my family support and encourage my child's continued participation in activities?

What if...

- **?** Your child is learning how to ride a bike and is having great difficulty. How do you support your child's learning?
- **?** Your child has an interest in dinosaurs and has difficulty changing focus. How do you support this interest while encouraging the development of new interests?
- **?** Your child is a member of a community group such as, beavers, brownies, cadets, etc. What new interests, skills, and knowledge is he/she developing?

Career Development for Young Children

What are my child's favorites?

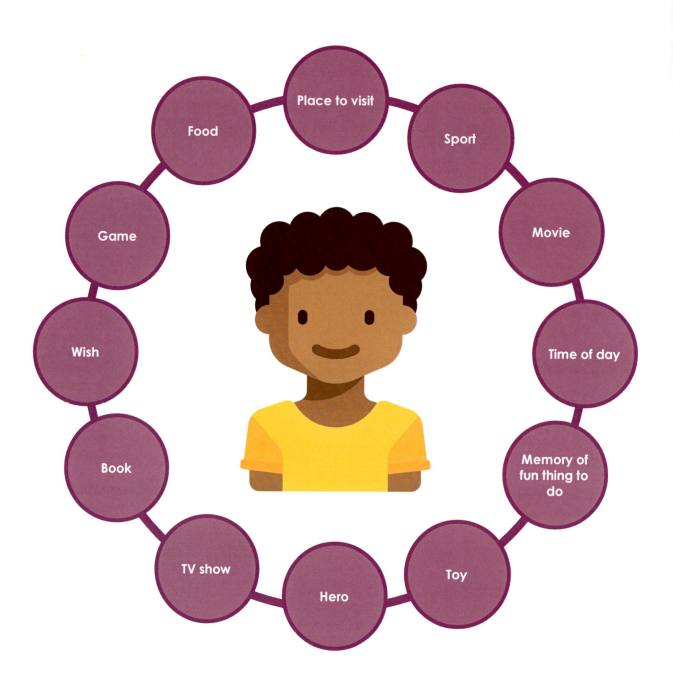

How do parents/guardians support and enhance children's development of healthy relationships?

At a glance

- Children learn appropriate social skills and ways to behave by observing and imitating the actions of others.
- Children's development of appropriate relationships is enhanced through practice.
- Parents model how to work and cooperate with others.
- The attitudes of parents towards diversity and individual differences will have a significant influence on a child's attitude.

Children's development of social behavior begins in infancy and continues into adulthood. The child's attachment and connectedness to parents during infancy and early childhood is critical to fostering a sense of security, self-reliance, self-confidence, and identity formation necessary for strong relationships throughout the lifespan.

Parents are the most important people in a child's life. In addition to providing the economic necessities of life, including shelter, food, and clothing, they offer warm, loving, and stable environments of emotional and social nurturance necessary for the growth and development of healthy relationships. Within the family units, children think, feel and act, and form values, interests, beliefs, and attitudes while becoming socialized into their culture. Children's first experiences with building healthy relationships essential to their emotional and overall psycholog-

Home life is very important and having opportunities for social interaction is important. (parent)

Career Development for Young Children 23

Female — 4 years old

She enjoys going to restaurants and watching movies with her family.

ical health occur within the family structure. Their development of social behavior is influenced by the nature of parents' interactions, actions, and responses in social environments. Thus, parents' behavior is a powerful teacher and can positively influence children's behavior. Parent who participated in our study talked about the importance of the influence of positive role models, mentors, and family values.

Another key ingredient for sustaining healthy relationships is the development of early, close friendships with peers who offer children opportunities for play in both structured and unstructured environments. Through play, children: develop self-knowledge; learn the rules of play; and master new skills that contribute to feelings of competence, self-confidence, and independence. As friendships become more important, children spend less time with parents and more with peers. They begin to think of 'we' as opposed to 'I'. As children develop relationships, they begin to compare and contrast their interests and talents with those of their peers. During later primary years, children become aware that there are opinions and views of the world that are different from their families. They begin to understand the perspective of others and learn how to manage conflict and negotiate differences. Parents in our study recognized the importance of positive social skills, such as team work, cooperation, and problem-solving.

VIGNETTE

Malika's grandmother noticed that Malika was somewhat shy when she took her to different social settings. When they were at the small playground in the community, Malika was reluctant to talk to the other children and often ran behind Grandma. When Grandma mentioned this to Malika parents, they were keen on helping Malika overcome this. They looked for opportunities in the community and enrolled Malika in Brownies. Malika loves Brownies and looks forward to engagement in fun activities with other children such as crafts, camping and fields trips to various community places. Grandma has noticed that Malika is much more outgoing, seems to be happier, and engages more easily with children and adults.

VIGNETTE

Adam's Mom understands the importance of building relationships, so she makes an effort to ensure that Adam spends time with his grandparents. Adam's grandparents don't live very close, but he does get to see them every month. Grandad loves to cook and Adam has baked cookies and made pizza with him many times. Grandma loves singing and has taught Adam many songs. Mom understands how her parents teach Adam many life lessons and provide him with opportunities to build healthy, loving relationships. Knowing that his grandparents really care about him boosts Adam's positive sense of self.

When children want to please their friends, peers' expectations of success and failure may influence children's willingness to take risks and pursue activities, even those that present challenges. Parents in our study noted the impact of peers as role models in the development of relationships.

As children begin to participate in out-of-school activities, they expand their worlds beyond their homes. Appropriate social behavior is important for effective engagement with others in all contexts, including workplaces. Parents in our study noted the impact of exposure to a variety of rich experiences in many different social settings on the development of relationships, healthy self-concepts, positive attitudes, and social competence for school, work, and life.

Children need role models. They need to see people in work roles. All outdoors activities are important. Children need to be active. (parent)

Female — 6 years old

She has to clean her room by herself. She likes the iPad, she wants to be a singer, and she has to decide on which friends to have over.

Career Development for Young Children 25

Female — 4 years old

Family is cooking supper; Mom is cooking, Dad is helping with the vegetables.

Children need opportunities to learn structure, to learn to follow routines, and get along in different settings with different people. (parent)

Extracurricular activities are important to support physical development and social development... Increases social awareness as they provide opportunity for her to integrate into many different settings and with different people. (parent)

I can decide to have friends over. (child)

Something to think about...

1. How do I model appropriate social behavior?
   - Do I talk to my child about appropriate and inappropriate social behavior?
   - Do I talk to my child about how to work and play cooperatively in a group?

2. How do I support my child in developing healthy relationships with others?
   - Do I encourage my child to express his/her feelings in an appropriate way?
   - Do I provide my child with opportunities to engage with other children and adults?

3. How do I model problem-solving strategies?

What if...

- Your child tries out for a role in a variety show or as a member of a team and is not chosen, but his best friend is. How do you want your child to respond?
- You and your child observe another child who is excluded from a game on the playground? How do you want your child to respond?
- Your child invites a friend to your house for a play date. This friend starts misusing your child's favorite toy. How do you want your child to respond?

How do parents/guardians support and empower children to adjust to change, make decisions, and solve problems?

At a glance

- Coping and adapting to change, making decisions, and problem-solving are skills that can be learned.
- Parents can make a positive difference in empowering children to manage change, make decisions, and problem-solve.
- Learning to deal effectively with change, to make decisions and problem-solve increases children's control over situations, and can reduce anxiety and stress.
- Children cope better with change and engage in decision-making and problem-solving when they feel safe and secure, and are supported through open communication.
- Keeping routines (mealtimes, bedtimes, etc.) during times of change helps children cope.
- Children learn to cope with change by exploring and trying out new interests.
- Early preparation and knowledge of strategies, supports, and resources support children in coping effectively with change, decision-making, and problem-solving.
- By providing opportunities to practice these skills, parents enable children to become more skilled at adapting to change, decision-making, and problem-solving.
- Introduce problem-solving and decision-making opportunities through play and fun activities.

Young children are creative; they enjoy solving problems and learning to adapt to changing situations and events. They observe, imitate, and mirror their parents' everyday problem-solving and decision-making skills.

Ability to change, make decisions, problem-solve, adapt to changing environments, and bounce back from setbacks (resiliency) are highly connected with self-efficacy, self-confidence, overall well-being, persistence, and self-motivation.

While planted in early childhood, the seeds of resiliency need to be nurtured throughout middle childhood and adolescence. How children engage in change and everyday decision-making and prob-

28   The Early Years

lem-solving will impact their future selves.

In our study, parents reflected that children are capable of having choices, making decisions and solving problems on their own. Most parents indicated that children like to be independent or at least have choices, and have opportunities to make decisions. Parents' responses varied with respect to their assessment of their children's confidence levels and ability to adapt to change.

Parents suggested various strategies to support their children's ongoing development, decision-making, problem-solving and resiliency as they journey through school, work, and careers. Parents noted that they generally give children choices, for example, over the clothes they wear and snack foods they eat. Many parents in our study noted that before change occurs they give children plenty of advance notice, and support them through the change while providing positive reinforcement. Parents can reassure their children and encourage them as they problem-solve by helping them break the problem or decision into small manageable steps. Opportunities for play enable children to experiment, explore, and gain a sense of hope which helps them to be proactive in creating their future. Young children's hopes, dreams, goals, aspirations, and values are key ingredients of education and career development.

However, sometimes children find themselves in situations that overwhelm them. On such occasions, they may hesitate, struggle, and fail, but with compassion, love, and support of their parents and family, they can recover. This support and encouragement will be an essential ingredient in the development of resilience.

The five year old adapts really well. There was no interruption when she went to kindergarten. She loves going to school and was so proud of that accomplishment. (parent)

Male — 6 years old

He wants to train dragons (saw it on You Tube).

She will select from food choices that I give her. I think that it is good that she is able to make choices and look at her options. (parent)

Transitions are difficult. For the first few weeks of back to school, he struggles to adjust. I focus on the positives of the situations. I help him look ahead on what is going to occur and to keep moving. (parent)

In our study, some parents commented that their children experienced difficulty adapting to change and may hesitate, struggle, and fail. The majority of parents believed that their children have high levels of resiliency and will do their best in difficult situations, even after making mistakes, will try again and bounce back from challenges.

Sometimes parents want to shield their children from possible failure in decision-making and problem-solving — they may even step in and

Career Development for Young Children 29

I try to teach him about what he is going to learn from the situation and give him positive reinforcement for being able to do it. I talk to him about the new skills that he has learned and how he can help others now who are in those situations. (parent)

She is more hesitant. She looks to us for guidance. We do encourage her to make her own decisions and will guide her to do that by helping her look at her options. (parent)

She is adaptable. We just tell her it is a part of life. (parent)

complete the task for the child. Parents can encourage children to learn from their errors and become less fearful of mistakes. A child who is comfortable with making mistakes will engage more willingly in problem-solving strategies.

There is great overlap between adaptability, high self-efficacy, a supportive environment, resiliency, and overall well-being. None of these ingredients are static; they change over time and are influenced by family, school, peers, and larger community.

VIGNETTE

The Barrett family is expecting a new baby. Baby Bailey will be a sister for five year old Braden. They know that this new addition is going to change their lives and they need to prepare themselves and Braden. The Barretts know that advance knowledge and preparation is important in dealing with change. Braden has been helping to set up a space for Bailey to sleep, deciding on toys that he can share with Bailey, and listing ways that he can help when Bailey comes home. The Barretts have been reading books about new babies to Braden and taking him shopping to prepare for Bailey's arrival. Braden is happy to be a helpful big brother.

VIGNETTE

Maggie is only six years old and she has been making choices since she was three. Maggie's Mom and her Grandmother and Pop believe that Maggie will be better prepared to make big choices when she is older, if she has lots of practice making little, appropriate choices when she is younger. Maggie is given a choice over her snacks: "Maggie, do you want crackers and cheese or apple slices this morning?" Maggie is given a choice over clothing: "Maggie, which of these sweaters do you want to wear today?" Maggie is also given a choice at playtime, and with helping out around the house. Her Mom and grandparents know that providing Maggie with choices will increase her sense of responsibility, and her ability to make decisions throughout her life.

Sometimes he is resistant to change and struggles with the thought of it. But when the change happens he is okay. We prepare him ahead of time. Let him know that the change is coming and what to expect. We don't spring change on him. (parent)

Male — 8 years old

He likes playing games and his Dad goes downstairs to make breakfast.

Career Development for Young Children 31

Something to think about...

1. What decisions do we make, and what problems do we solve, as a family?
   - Does everyone participate in the process?
   - How do we arrive at decisions?

2. What decisions does my child make on his/her own?
   - Does my child make his/her own decisions regarding clothing, food, and choice of entertainment (age-appropriate)?

3. How does my child solve problems?
   - Does he/she attempt a solution of his/her own?
   - Does he/she look for support from others?
   - Does he/she persist when a solution is not obvious?

What if...

- ? Your child's birthday is coming up and decisions have to be made regarding a party, including food, invitations, gifts, etc. How do you include your child in the planning and decision-making?
- ? Your family has to relocate because of work. How do you prepare your family for this change? How do you support your child during the change?
- ? You are running late and your child needs to get dressed to go with you. How do you avoid putting undue stress on your child?

How do parents/guardians support and empower children to participate in family and community life?

At a glance

- Helping others gives children a sense of accomplishment and pride.
- Through engagement with their families and communities, children gain knowledge about aspects of work and the benefits of team work.
- Children's self-esteem and self-efficacy are enhanced through involvement and from the appreciation they receive for their contribution.
- Children learn the value of helping others in many ways, including completion of tasks and chores, and engagement in volunteer activities.
- Engagement in chores and tasks is important as a way of understanding responsibility, participating in leadership roles, and increasing self-esteem and a feeling of belonging.

Children develop their identity as they participate in family and community life by trying things out, and experiencing the joy of becoming engaged in activities. These experiences help children figure out who they really are and who they want to become. Furthermore, their self-efficacy increases as they experience success and accomplish their goals.

Parent participants in our study indicated the importance of children's contribution to family and community. They talked easily about the long-term benefits of children having chores and tasks at home, as well as engagement in volunteer activities. Although some parents noted that their children did better with the completion of chores if they were rewarded, the majority of parents recognized children's lifelong lessons from completion of chores. These lessons include life

Female — 8 years old

She would like to work with her Dad's company and own it. Dad owns his own construction company.

Career Development for Young Children 33

Female — 5 years old

She is an artist like her Uncle Johnny.

Male — 6 years old

When he gets bigger he wants to build houses like his Dad.

My Mom made a list of chores for me and my brother. It's important to help around the house and clean my room. (child)

I help clean my room. I help bake cookies. I help my little and big sister. (child)

skills, values, responsibility, respect for other members of the family, independence, persistence (hard work), organization, and sense of accomplishment. Parents reported that children also learn the value of helping others, realize that they can make a positive difference in people's lives, experience feelings of belonging to the family and community, and begin a possible lifetime of giving back to family and community.

A limited number of children talked about

I have chores and I get paid $10.00. (child)

I have to clean my room on Fridays; I get $5.00. (child)

the monetary reward which they received for completing tasks and chores. However, most child participants in our study readily talked about their contributions to their families. Their responses indicated that completion of tasks and chores at home is very much a part of family life. Children who completed tasks and chores felt proud that their contributions were important in helping the family.

Most parents indicated that their children have responsibilities for age-appropriate chores and tasks at home. The nature of these responsibilities included such things as: making beds, putting dishes in the sink, cleaning up after play, and helping with younger siblings and pets. In some instances, parents reported that children have reservations towards chores or tasks, and they often needed encouragement and support for completion. Children, ages three to eight years, readily identified typical age-appropriate tasks and chores for which they had responsibility such as: helping with pets, tidying up, setting tables, and other light household chores. Some children identified completion of homework/school work as a task or chore.

Chores teach responsibility; teaches life skills. Effort is important, and they [the children] need to contribute. (parent)

He learns to stick with tasks that he does not enjoy. He learns they are not so bad once he gets into them. He learns not to complain about tasks. He learns that he gets better at things the more he does them. And, he learns to use his time well. (parent)

They learn to work towards a goal and to reap the benefits from their efforts. (parent)

VIGNETTE

At the Malik's house, Samira is expected to participate in doing small chores. Samira and her Dad wrote chores on pieces of paper and she has to select two chores each week from the chore box. She gets to select chores such as, setting the table, picking up her toys, and walking the dog. Dad likes for Samira to help with the family chores, and he knows that when she is productive, she learns to take responsibility and feels like an important member of the family.

Career Development for Young Children

Something to think about...

1. How does my child contribute to our family?
   - How do I involve my child in sharing the chores?
   - How do I encourage my child's efforts?

2. How does my child contribute in his/her community, including preschool and school?
   - How do I encourage my child to make contributions to his/her school and community by donating or giving his/her time?

What if...

- Your community initiates a clean-up campaign. How do you support your child's engagement in this project?
- There is an upcoming fall fair in your community. How do you support your child's engagement in this project?
- After a meal there is a lot of clean up required. How do you engage your child to share in the process?

36   The Early Years

How do parents/guardians influence children's aspirations for future selves?

At a glance

- From a very early age, children have a vision of how they see themselves in the future. Their aspirations and dreams are expressed through means such as role-playing, dress-up centers, art, and verbal expression.
- Children who are supported in their dreams and visions for the future are more likely to explore a diverse range of future career options, and not prematurely rule out specific career choices.
- TV, media, games, and significant events often influence children's aspirations for present and future roles.
- It is important for children to be exposed to positive role models, mentors, and a wide variety of experiences across diverse environments and settings.
- Children's aspirations for future selves change frequently and reflect their experiences and interests, the life roles of parents and significant others, and activities and roles based both in reality and fantasy.
- Children's aspirations for roles based in reality range from doctor, nurse, truck driver, teacher, sports player, etc., and reflect their experiences and exposure to careers of family members and other significant adults, such as teachers, doctors, and community workers.

Young children play, experiment with new things, and interact with their parents, siblings, and peers while growing and developing a sense of themselves and their world. With warm, supportive, and compassionate environments, they learn to make decisions, solve problems, and develop positive beliefs about themselves. This sense of self in the present will expand into their future selves, their aspirations, and goals, which are very important in career development.

Children's hopes and dreams for their futures are fuelled by their experiences and relationships in the present. Parents are central to their children's present and future selves. Your reassurances and focus on effort, strengths, positive accomplishments, and progress, foster and sustain a sense of hope and optimism for the future.

According to parent participants in our study, young chil-

> **Children's dreams for possible selves include both fantasy and reality aspirations.**

Career Development for Young Children   37

Every kid dreams about when they are bigger. When I was a child I wanted to be a rock star. My children talk about what they want to be. It changes from time to time based on their experiences and their interests. (parent)

My daughter went to the dentist with Brownies and she talks about being a dentist. My seven year old son likes to build things and he talks about being a carpenter like his Dad. (parent)

I want to be a teacher because I really like school and I want to be around children. (child)

I would like to teach in and own my own day care; I love children. (child)

I want to be a marine biologist because I love sharks. (child)

When I am bigger I will be a princess. (child)

I encourage her with all of her dreams. (parent)

They are very much aware of their gender and what they are strong at. I see gender identity with choice of toys and she likes dressing up. (parent)

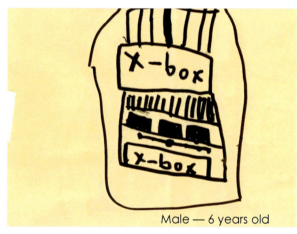

Male — 6 years old

He wants to work at an Xbox store to sell them. He likes Xbox games and Dad wants him to sell Xboxes.

dren often talk about their hopes and dreams for the future. Parents noted that these aspirations change often and are influenced by parents' life roles and activities, children's interests and experiences, and TV and media.

Parents did not comment on the influence of school experiences on their children's future selves. However, several children dreamed of roles, such as teacher, bus driver, and school nurse.

Children represented their aspirations and dreams for future selves through their stories, drawings, and paintings. During the focus groups, children were asked questions related to their future selves and reasons for their interests and the main source(s) of influence. They frequently envisioned future roles as enjoyable and chose roles that they knew something about.

Male — 4 years old

His interests are in Batman, Spiderman and Mario Brothers. Interested in becoming a better Batman or Spiderman.

Children's descriptions for future roles were diverse and varied from fantasy to reality, for example, princess, dancer, playing Minecraft, doctor, nurse, carpenter, and police officer. Fantasy roles were more often aspirations of younger children.

Most parents recognized the importance of providing their children with opportunities to explore diverse possibilities and interesting options for their future selves. They encouraged their children to imagine many possibilities. A small number of parents wanted their children to reflect on income and lifestyle when considering their future aspirations. Children's aspirations often reflected more traditional roles and adhered to stereotypical gender roles, for example, five and six year olds most frequently dreamed of being doctors, teachers, or police officers.

During the focus group sessions, children were asked questions related to reasons for their career interests or the main source(s) of influence on their future selves. Their representations of their future selves included roles of their 'idols' and 'heroes' in media, TV, books, etc. (e.g., a doctor like Dr. McStuffin, go to Spain and learn Spanish like Dora.)

I want to be a professional soccer or hockey player. I am a big fan of soccer and sports. (child)

I want to be in the marine forces like Dad. (child)

I would love to travel all around the world, like Paris, drawing and designing buildings and cities. I like to work with lots of technology. (child)

Children's aspirations of future roles were also related to their current activities/sports (a hockey player, a video game designer, a car engineer).

Children's awareness and understanding of specific responsibilities of work roles influenced their depictions of future selves. One six-year-old child explained that he wanted to be a construction worker because he likes to build houses and likes "building stuff with Legos." Another

VIGNETTE

Last month when the road was being repaired outside Max's home, Max decided that when he grew up he was going to be a truck driver, like one of the workers he saw. Just this past week, Max went on a field trip to the bakery, and has now decided he will be a cook when he grows up — he wants his own apron and measuring cups. Dad realizes that Max's dreams for the future change often. He lets Max talk about his dreams, and explore them through play and real life experiences.

Female — 8 years old

She likes dancing and when she grows up she wants to be a dancer.

child described his dream of becoming a chef based on knowledge that "To be a chef you have to ring the bell, work the stove, and learn how to cook." Occupations of parents and significant adults in children's lives were frequently cited and also influenced their own future aspirations (e.g., a truck driver, a teacher, a carpenter, a marine biologist).

Many children envisioned a future with multiple roles. Some of these roles included dual professional roles while other future selves comprised a professional career, a parent, and/or a leisure role. Other children were aware of technology and expressed a future working with it.

Something to think about...

1. What opportunities exist for my child to interact with peers from diverse backgrounds?
2. What opportunities do I provide for my child to be exposed to a diverse range of role models in movies, books, and other resources?
3. How do I monitor the games, books, TV programs, and videos to which my child is exposed?
4. Does my child have opportunities to engage in imaginative play in a variety of settings?

What if...

- You are watching a movie or reading a book with your child. How do you engage your child in a discussion about the diverse roles of various characters?
- Your child frequently engages in dress-up of characters (from real-life and fantasy). How do you engage with your child in this type of play?
- You take your child on outings, road trips, and excursions. How do you use these opportunities to expose your child to diverse experiences?

Career Development for Young Children 41

How do parents/guardians enhance children's knowledge of diverse work roles in families and communities?

At a glance

- Children learn very early that work is a very important part of life.
- Community helpers and workers are part of children's everyday lives.
- Children become knowledgeable about work and workers very early in life through exposure at home and in the community.
- Parents' discussions with their children about various workers lead to increased curiosity and knowledge.
- Exposure to occupations and careers occurs via a variety of media, including, books, videos, field trips, and guest speakers.
- Play is a child's work. Through play, children explore many different roles.

Children are aware of work concepts and roles at a very early age. They are naturally curious and are interested in what the adults do within their families and communities. Parents, uncles, aunts, grandparents, close family friends, and community members present a wide range of careers, jobs, and occupations. The media, including television, expose them to jobs and occupations, sometimes accurate and other times less so. Children become motivated and interested in these jobs and occupations. They frequently act out roles in their play- and fantasy-based activities.

By the time children begin school, they have had wide exposure to diverse work roles. They are beginning to develop interests, formulate attitudes, and express their preferences. As they grow and mature cognitively, they begin to grasp and understand the interrelationships among the various jobs and occupations.

Parents support their children by introducing them to those jobs and occupations within the family and larger community. They counteract any stereotyping that appears in the media, on television, or in everyday conversations. Children learn from the adults they observe and often imitate their behaviours, including respect of the diversity of work and for the people who execute this work.

In our study, parents reported that children have a general awareness of parents' work roles and this awareness increases in specificity as children age. Parents see children as interested

They know the basics of our work — I am a firefighter and carpenter, and Mom is a nurse. They know that I help put out fires and build things, and that Mom gives medicine and needles. (parent)

42   The Early Years

Mom is an engineer. Dad has three jobs, army, and police. He is also a cub leader. (child)

I will be a veterinarian to help animals. (child)

I want to be a rock star and be famous and have people run to me. (child)

I want to be a musician. I love to play the piano. (child)

and curious about their work. Younger children are able to name their parents' as well as other family members' careers, for example, teacher, doctor, truck driver, and are aware of basic work roles.

Some parents reported that they talk to their children about their work. The depth of conversations varied and discussions with older children revealed more details regarding specific work tasks and responsibilities. Many parents indicated that their children had been to their place of work and that the visits have been positive experiences for their children. Furthermore, children increased their awareness of diverse work roles from exposure of workers in their immediate environments. A daycare educator reported, for example, that while construction occurred on their road outside their building, children were very curious and interested in knowing what the various workers did, such as the backhoe driver, the engineer, and the flag person.

Children also reported that they have learned about work from various television programs they have watched and from social media. Various visitors and speakers within early learning centres and school environments also increased students' knowledge of diverse workers. For example, one primary school teacher reported that every Friday she provided time for a parent to share knowledge of their hobbies or work with the children.

Parents also reported that their children were often interested in the work of characters they read about in books or saw in movies and on TV.

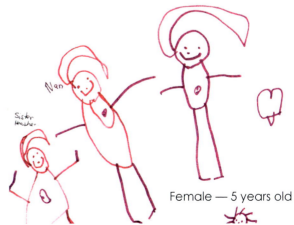

Female — 5 years old

She loves helping her Grandma and Mom make cookies and cake.

Career Development for Young Children   43

VIGNETTE

Terry made many trips with her Mom and Dad to the supermarket, the post office, the town hall, and other places in the community. Many times Terry did not want to go, but Mom and Dad recognize the benefits of visiting and becoming familiar with these places. Mom and Dad know that Terry learns about appropriate behavior in each of these settings, and gets to see the routines and structure in each place. She also gets to interact with the workers and see the diversity of work that takes place. Mom and Dad feel that these experiences have a positive influence on Terry's social development and increase her knowledge of workers in the community.

She likes cats and she and Mom take care of the garden.

Undoubtedly, exposure to diverse roles both in the media and through familial, school, and community experiences broadened children's understanding and knowledge of work.

Parents' responses reflected support of the importance of early exposure to a variety of occupations, jobs, and work. Parents believed that exposure to diverse occupations occurs at preschool and primary school through awareness of workers in their communities, and from parents who share knowledge and information regarding their work. The majority of parents believed that children should be learning about the world of work prior to school and during primary grades, and feel that it is important for young children to be knowledgeable about workers in their communities.

Children represented their knowledge of parents' and others' work through stories, painting and drawing during the focus groups. Generally, children's knowledge of parents' and other adults' work ranged from awareness that they work, to naming the place of work and the specific occupation, and providing some details of the work. Specificity increased with age of children.

Children's perception of the purpose of work generally focused on the need to make money to pay for the necessities of life. Young children's responses often put themselves at the center of why parents and others needed to work. These included buying a home and paying for vehicles, food, vacations, and extras such as toys. In addition, children's responses reflected a degree of awareness of parents' commitment of time to work, varying attitudes of parents towards work, and the stress of work. Younger children (ages five to eight years) talked about the 'time' factor of work. Older children (5-8 and 7-8) demonstrated a greater awareness of parents' work, and their feelings and attitudes about work.

At a very young age, we should be talking about the occupations that we see in the community. Earlier we talk about it the better. The more children know about the possible occupations, the earlier they can start and learn new skills and learn about themselves. (parent)

Three people work, my Grandma works at church and the hall. Mom works at yoga. Dad works far away; he's a truck driver. (child)

Grandma and Pop work to make money to buy me toys. (child)

Mom works at the hospital. She is very tired after working nights. Dad works at electrical company installing phones. (child)

Ages	Children's Awareness of Work
3 and 4	• Grandma and Pop work to make money to buy me toys. • They go to work to make money to go shopping to buy food. • Mom and Dad work all the time. • Work is not fun because Mom and Dad have to go.
5 and 6	• They work because it is important, so they can get rich. If they don't work, they can't get rich. • People work to give us food, clothes, and toys. • People go to work to make money to buy BMX bike. • My Dad does not like going to work. • Mom works at a desk, I would not like that.
7 and 8	• People work to get money to buy us food, to keep me in my house, and buy shampoo. • People work to get money to go on vacation. • Depends whether people have kids as to whether they like work. They might miss the kids and want to go home. • I think people like work; some get frustrated, and some don't. • Sometime people get fired because they don't do the job well.

Career Development for Young Children   45

Something to think about...

1. Who are the workers and helpers that are a part of my child's everyday life?
   - How do I engage my child in conversation about the work of people in the family and in the community?
   - What does my child know about my occupation, place of work, and what I do?
   - What does my child know about the careers of various family members?

2. How does my child interact with the workers and helpers in his/her neighborhood?
   - Is my child aware of the diversity of workers in our neighborhood?
   - Is my child aware of the importance of various occupations to the wellbeing of others in the community?

What if...

- Your hours of work have to increase. How do you discuss this with your family?
- You take your child to shop at the farmers' market. What does your child know about the workers involved in getting food to the market?
- You have had a very frustrating day at work. How do you discuss this with your family?
- You are having major renovations completed on your home involving a number of workers such as, carpenter, plumber, electrician, and decorator. How do you use this experience to increase your child's knowledge of various work roles?

Highlights

Parents/guardians...

- Help children feel safe and secure.

- Build nurturing, loving, and caring relationships with children.

- Support children in building positive relationships with others.

- Participate in fun activities (e.g., read and play games and sports) as a family.

- Recognize children's efforts and achievements, and provide support when needed.

- Enhance children's confidence by encouraging them to try new things and to be open to change.

- Encourage children to develop and recognize strengths, interests, and abilities, and think positively about themselves.

- Provide children with opportunities for imaginative play.

- Monitor the games, books and media in which children engage.

- Encourage children to imagine many possibilities for future selves.

- Provide choices to encourage children to make decisions (e.g., clothing, snacks, toys, and activities).

- Help children set and accomplish appropriate goals.

- Provide opportunities for children to contribute in their home and community.

- Model acceptable ways to resolve conflict and deal with frustration.

- Expose children to the diverse range of workers who are part of their everyday lives, including the work of other family members and friends.

- Encourage exploration of a variety of occupations through books, TV, media, games, and other activities.

- Discuss work with children, including place of work and some job tasks and responsibilities.

- Are role models.

Note to parents/guardians

In the early years of development, children learn about their world, develop relationships, and try on different 'roles' through play. Children by nature are curious and creative. Play helps them develop new ideas, concepts, and ways of doing things; they learn rules, break rules, and sometimes adopt new rules. Through play they figure out how things work, what doesn't work, and they often fail and try again.

You help in your child's developmental process by providing an encouraging, caring, and supportive environment. You foster and nurture your child's imagination, creativity, curiosity, love of learning, and self-efficacy.

Additionally, children learn through observations of your behaviors and responses. You are models of many essential career-related skills, including decision-making, problem-solving, adapting to change, risk taking and social and communication skills. Your reassurances and focus on effort, strengths, and positive accomplishments foster and sustain a sense of hope and optimism for the future.

You provide opportunities for children to engage in chores and activities that instill a sense of responsibility, mastery, and pride. Children learn valuable life lessons from engagement in chores and activities (e.g., life skills, responsibility, independence, and persistence).

As parents, you also influence your child's attitudes towards various work roles by supporting and encouraging exploration of a diverse range of careers and possibilities for future selves.

You are indeed the most influential person in the development of your young child. It is our hope that you find the ideas and suggestions presented in this guide helpful in the early years of your child's career development.

References

Bandura, A., Barbaranelli, C., Caprara, G. V., & Pastorelli, C. (2001). Self-efficacy beliefs as shapers of children's aspirations and career trajectories. *Child Development, 72(1),* 187-206.

Bandura, A., Barbaranelli, C., Caprara, G. V., & Pastorelli, C. (1999). Self-efficacy pathways to childhood depression. *Journal of Personality and Social Psychology, 76(2),* 258-269.

Bandura, A., Barbaranelli, C., Caprara, G. V., & Pastorelli, C. (1996). Multifaceted impact of self-efficacy beliefs on academic functioning. *Child Development, 67(3),* 1206-1222.

Blustein, D. L., Schultheiss, D. E .P., & Flum, H. (2004). Toward a relational perspective of the psychology of careers and working: A social constructionist analysis. *Journal of Vocational Behavior, 64,* 423-440.

Cinamon, R. G., & Dan, O. (2010). Parental attitudes toward preschoolers' career education: A mixed-method study. *Journal of Career Development, 37,* 519-540.

Gottfredson, L. S. (1981). Circumscription and compromise: A developmental theory of occupational aspirations. *Journal of Counseling Psychology, 28(6),* 545-579.

Hartung, P., Porfeli, E. J., & Vondracek, F. W. (2008). Career adaptability in childhood. *Career Development Quarterly, 57(1),* 63-74.

Hartung, P. J., Porfeli, E. J., & Vondracek, F. W. (2005). Child vocational development: A review and reconsideration. *Journal of Vocational Behaviour, 66,* 385–419.

Helwig, A. A. (2008). From Childhood to adulthood: A 15 year longitudinal career development study. *Career Development Quarterly, 57(1),* 38-50.

Helwig, A. A. (1998). Occupational aspirations of a longitudinal sample from second to sixth grade. *Journal of Career Development, 24(4),* 247–265.

Herr, E. L., Cramer, S. H., & Niles, S. G. (2004). *Career guidance and counseling through the lifespan: Systematic approaches* (6th ed.). Boston, MA: Allyn & Bacon.

Keller, B. K., & Whiston, S. C. (2008). The role of parental influences on young adolescents' career development. *Journal of Career Assessment, 16,* 198-217.

Magnuson, C. S., & Starr, M. (2000). How early is too early to begin life career planning? The importance of the elementary school years. *Journal of Career Development, 27(2),* 89–101.

Markus, H., & Nurius, P. (1986). Possible selves. *American Psychologist, 41(9),* 954-969.

Masten, A. S. (2014). Global perspectives on resilience in children and youth. *Child Development, 85(1),* 6-20.

Niles, S. G. & Harris-Bowlsbey, J. (2017). *Career development interventions.* (5th ed.). Toronto: Pearson.

Palladino S., & Stead, G. B. (2004). Childhood career development scale: Scale construction and psychometric properties. *Journal of Career Assessment, 12(2),* 113–134.

Porfeli, E. J., Hartung, P. J., & Vondracek, F. W. (2008). Children's vocational development: A research rationale. *Career Development Quarterly, 57,* 25-37.

Savickas, M. L. (2012). A paradigm for career intervention in the 21st century. *Journal of Counseling and Development, 90,* 13–19.

Schultheiss, D. E. P. (2007). The emergence of a relational cultural paradigm for vocational psychology. *International Journal of Education and Vocational Guidance, 7,* 191-201.

Schultheiss, D. E. P., Palma, T. V., & Manzi, A. J. (2005). Career development in middle childhood: A qualitative inquiry. *Career Development Quarterly, 53,* 246-262.

Starr, M. F. (1996). Comprehensive guidance and systematic educational and career planning: Why a K-12 approach? *Journal of Career Development, 23(1),* 9–22.

Trice, A., Hughes, M., Odom, C., Woods, K., & McClellan, N. (1995). The origins of children's career aspirations: IV. Testing hypotheses from four theories. *The Career Development Quarterly, 43,* 307-322.

Watson, M., & McMahon, M. (2008). Children's career development: Metaphorical images of theory, research & practice. *Career Development* Quarterly, *57(1),* 75-83.

Watson, M., & McMahon, M. (2005). Children's career development: A research review from a learning perspective. *Journal of Vocational* Behavior, *67(2),* 119-132.

Watson, M. B., & McMahon, M. (2004). Children's career development: A meta-theoretical perspective. *Australian Journal of Career Development, 13,* 7–11.

Whiston, S. C., & Keller, B. K. (2004). The influences of the family of origin on career development: A review and analysis. *The Counseling Psychologist, 32,* 493-568.

Young, R. A., Valach, L., & Marshall, S. K. (2007). Parents and youth co-constructing career. In V. Shorokov & W. Patton (Eds.), *Career development in childhood and adolescence* (pp. 643–657). Rotterdam: Sense Publishers.

Acknowledgements

We would like to acknowledge a number of people and organizations who contributed to the completion of this project. Firstly, we would like to thank the children, staff, and parents from the preschools, daycares and Family Resource Centres, from Newfoundland and Labrador, who participated in this study. Secondly, we would like to thank the children (grades Kindergarten to three), administrators (both at Board and school level), educators, and parents of the Newfoundland and Labrador English School District who participated in this study.

We would like to extend our appreciation to Sandra Taylor and Mary Kelsey, our dedicated and highly competent research assistants, who made this experience truly enjoyable and meaningful. They were integral to all phases of this research from data collection (dissemination of quantitative surveys and facilitation of focus groups) and data analyses, to the completion of deliverables.

We also thank Ms. Alison Carr and Ms. Allyson MacNeill-Hajek for their professional design.

We are indebted to CERIC for making this project possible through their funding, encouragement, and ongoing support. As well, we thank Memorial University of Newfoundland for their financial and administrative support. We are particularly appreciative of the special efforts of Norman Valdez, Sharon Ferris, and Riz Ibrahim on this project – a sincere 'thank you'.

Research Team

Principal Investigators
Mildred Cahill, PhD
Faculty of Education
Memorial University of Newfoundland

Edith Furey, PhD
Faculty of Education
Memorial University of Newfoundland

Funders

CERIC
Foundation House
2 St. Clair Avenue East
Suite 300
Toronto, ON
M4T 2T5
www.ceric.ca

Research Assistants

Sandra Taylor, MEd
Conception Bay South, NL

Mary Kelsey, MEd
St. John's, NL

Faculty of Education
Memorial University of Newfoundland
St. John's, NL
A1B 3X8
www.mun.ca